Timeless
Christening Sets

Whether you want to knit a christening outfit for a girl or a boy, you've found the ideal designs right here! For a little princess, create the Sweet Snowflakes or Sugar & Spice. Each includes a gown, bonnet, and booties. For that lovable new guy in your life, Bouncing Boy has a romper, cap, and booties. When wearing these adorable designs, that special baby will be picture perfect on the big day!

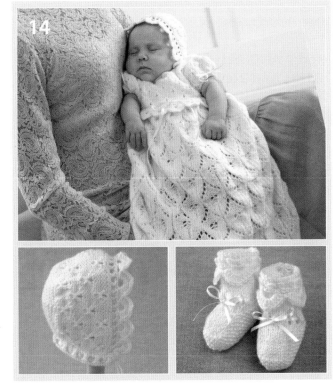

LEISURE ARTS, INC. • Little Rock, Arkansas

Sweet Snowflakes ◼◼◼◻ INTERMEDIATE

Size: Newborn to 3 months

MATERIALS
Light Weight Yarn 🔵**3**🔵
[7 ounces, 575 yards
(198 grams, 525 meters) per skein]:
   2 skeins
24" (61 cm) Circular knitting needles,
   sizes 6 (4 mm) **and** 7 (4.5 mm) **or**
   sizes needed for gauge
16" (40.5 cm) Circular knitting needle, size 6 (4 mm)
Straight knitting needles, 6 (4 mm)
Markers
Point protectors
7/16" (11 mm) Buttons - 4
1/4" (7 mm) wide Ribbon - 24" (61 cm)
Sewing needle and matching thread
Tapestry needle

GAUGE: In Stockinette Stitch,
   with smaller size needles,
   22 sts and 28 rows = 4" (10 cm)

Techniques used:
• Knit increase (**Figs. 5a & b, page 36**)
• Adding new sts (**Figs. 8a & b, page 37**)
• K1 tbl (**Fig. 1, page 35**)
• YO (**Figs. 4a & b, page 36**)
• K2 tog (**Fig. 9, page 37**)
• K2 tog tbl (**Fig. 10, page 37**)
• K3 tog (**Fig. 11, page 37**)
• SSK (**Figs. 15a-c, page 38**)
• P2 tog (**Fig. 12, page 38**)
• P2 tog tbl (**Fig. 13, page 38**)
• Slip 1 as if to **knit**, K2 tog, PSSO (**Figs. 16a & b, page 38**)
• Slip 2 tog as if to **knit**, K1, P2SSO (**Figs. 17a & b, page 39**)

When instructed to slip a stitch, always slip as if to **purl**, unless otherwise instructed.

GOWN
SKIRT
BAND
With 24" (61 cm) larger size circular knitting needle, cast on 220 sts (*see Circular Knitting, page 35*), place marker to mark beginning of rnd (*see Markers, page 35*).

Rnd 1 (Right side)**:** (WYF slip 1, P1) around.

Rnd 2: (K1, P1) around.

Rnds 3 and 4: Knit around.

Rnds 5-12: Repeat Rnds 1-4 twice.

BODY
Change to 24" (61 cm) smaller size circular knitting needle.

Rnd 1: (YO, SSK, K 17, K2 tog, YO, K1 tbl) around.

Rnd 2 AND ALL EVEN-NUMBERED RNDS THRU Rnd 26: Knit around.

Rnd 3: ★ K1 tbl, YO, SSK, K 15, (K2 tog, YO) twice; repeat from ★ around.

Rnd 5: ★ (YO, SSK) twice, K 13, (K2 tog, YO) twice, K1; repeat from ★ around.

Rnd 7: K1, (YO, SSK) twice, K 11, (K2 tog, YO) twice, ★ K3, (YO, SSK) twice, K 11, (K2 tog, YO) twice; repeat from ★ around to last 2 sts, K2.

Rnd 9: K2, (YO, SSK) twice, K9, (K2 tog, YO) twice, ★ K5, (YO, SSK) twice, K9, (K2 tog, YO) twice; repeat from ★ around to last 3 sts, K3.

Front

Back

Rnd 11: K3, (YO, SSK) twice, K1, SSK, YO, K1, YO, K2 tog, K1, (K2 tog, YO) twice, ★ K7, (YO, SSK) twice, K1, SSK, YO, K1, YO, K2 tog, K1, (K2 tog, YO) twice; repeat from ★ around to last 4 sts, K4.

Rnd 13: K4, (YO, SSK) twice, K1, YO, slip 2 tog as if to **knit**, K1, P2SSO, YO, K1, (K2 tog, YO) twice, ★ K9, (YO, SSK) twice, K1, YO, slip 2 tog as if to **knit**, K1, P2SSO, YO, K1, (K2 tog, YO) twice; repeat from ★ around to last 5 sts, K5.

Rnd 15: K5, YO, SSK, YO, slip 1 as if to **knit**, K2 tog, PSSO, YO, K1, YO, K3 tog, YO, K2 tog, YO, ★ K 11, YO, SSK, YO, slip 1 as if to **knit**, K2 tog, PSSO, YO, K1, YO, K3 tog, YO, K2 tog, YO; repeat from ★ around to last 6 sts, K6.

Rnd 17: K6, (YO, SSK) twice, K1, (K2 tog, YO) twice, ★ K 13, (YO, SSK) twice, K1, (K2 tog, YO) twice; repeat from ★ around to last 7 sts, K7.

Rnd 19: ★ K2 tog, K5, YO, SSK, YO, slip 1 as if to **knit**, K2 tog, PSSO, YO, K2 tog, YO, K5, SSK, YO, K1, YO; repeat from ★ around.

Rnd 21: ★ K7, YO, SSK, YO, slip 1 as if to **knit**, K2 tog, PSSO, YO, K7, YO, slip 2 tog as if to **knit**, K1, P2SSO, YO; repeat from ★ around.

Rnd 23: Remove marker, K1, place marker, ★ K7, YO, slip 1 as if to **knit**, K2 tog, PSSO, YO, K7, SSK, YO, K1, YO, K2 tog; repeat from ★ around.

Rnd 25: K7, slip 2 tog as if to **knit**, K1, P2SSO, ★ K 19, slip 2 tog as if to **knit**, K1, P2SSO; repeat from ★ around to last 12 sts, K 12: 200 sts.

Rnd 27: Knit around to last 2 sts, slip last 2 sts onto right needle tip and remove marker, slip same 2 sts back onto left needle tip and place marker.

Rnds 28-34: Knit around.

Rnd 35: ★ YO, SSK, K 15, K2 tog, YO, K1 tbl; repeat from ★ around.

Rnd 36 AND ALL EVEN-NUMBERED RNDS THRU Rnd 58: Knit around.

Rnd 37: ★ K1 tbl, YO, SSK, K 13, (K2 tog, YO) twice; repeat from ★ around.

Rnd 39: ★ (YO, SSK) twice, K 11, (K2 tog, YO) twice, K1; repeat from ★ around.

Rnd 41: K1, (YO, SSK) twice, K9, (K2 tog, YO) twice, ★ K3, (YO, SSK) twice, K9, (K2 tog, YO) twice; repeat from ★ around to last 2 sts, K2.

Rnd 43: K2, (YO, SSK) twice, K1, SSK, YO, K1, YO, K2 tog, K1, (K2 tog, YO) twice, ★ K5, (YO, SSK) twice, K1, SSK, YO, K1, YO, K2 tog, K1, (K2 tog, YO) twice; repeat from ★ around to last 3 sts, K3.

Rnd 45: K3, (YO, SSK) twice, K1, YO, slip 2 tog as if to knit, K1, P2SSO, YO, K1, (K2 tog, YO) twice, ★ K7, (YO, SSK) twice, K1, YO, slip 2 tog as if to knit, K1, P2SSO, YO, K1, (K2 tog, YO) twice; repeat from ★ around to last 4 sts, K4.

Rnd 47: K4, YO, SSK, YO, slip 1 as if to knit, K2 tog, PSSO, YO, K1, YO, K3 tog, YO, K2 tog, YO, ★ K9, YO, SSK, YO, slip 1 as if to knit, K2 tog, PSSO, YO, K1, YO, K3 tog, YO, K2 tog, YO; repeat from ★ around to last 5 sts, K5.

Rnd 49: K5, (YO, SSK) twice, K1, (K2 tog, YO) twice, ★ K 11, (YO, SSK) twice, K1, (K2 tog, YO) twice; repeat from ★ around to last 6 sts, K6.

Rnd 51: ★ K2 tog, K4, YO, SSK, YO, slip 1 as if to knit, K2 tog, PSSO, YO, K2 tog, YO, K4, SSK, YO, K1, YO; repeat from ★ around.

Rnd 53: ★ K6, YO, SSK, YO, slip 1 as if to knit, K2 tog, PSSO, YO, K6, YO, slip 2 tog as if to knit, K1, P2SSO, YO; repeat from ★ around.

Rnd 55: Remove marker, K1, place marker, ★ K6, YO, slip 1 as if to knit, K2 tog, PSSO, YO, K6, SSK, YO, K1, YO, K2 tog; repeat from ★ around.

Rnd 57: K6, slip 2 tog as if to knit, K1, P2SSO, ★ K 17, slip 2 tog as if to knit, K1, P2SSO; repeat from ★ around to last 11 sts, K 11: 180 sts.

Rnd 59: Knit around to last 2 sts, slip last 2 sts onto right needle tip and remove marker, slip same 2 sts back onto left needle tip and place marker.

Rnds 60-66: Knit around.

Rnd 67: ★ YO, SSK, K 13, K2 tog, YO, K1 tbl; repeat from ★ around.

Rnd 68 AND ALL EVEN-NUMBERED RNDS THRU Rnd 88: Knit around.

Rnd 69: ★ K1 tbl, YO, SSK, K 11, (K2 tog, YO) twice; repeat from ★ around.

Rnd 71: ★ (YO, SSK) twice, K9, (K2 tog, YO) twice, K1; repeat from ★ around.

Rnd 73: K1, (YO, SSK) twice, K1, SSK, YO, K1, YO, K2 tog, K1, (K2 tog, YO) twice, ★ K3, (YO, SSK) twice, K1, SSK, YO, K1, YO, K2 tog, K1, (K2 tog, YO) twice; repeat from ★ around to last 2 sts, K2.

Rnd 75: K2, (YO, SSK) twice, K1, YO, slip 2 tog as if to knit, K1, P2SSO, YO, K1, (K2 tog, YO) twice, ★ K5, (YO, SSK) twice, K1, YO, slip 2 tog as if to knit, K1, P2SSO, YO, K1, (K2 tog, YO) twice; repeat from ★ around to last 3 sts, K3.

Rnd 77: K3, YO, SSK, YO, slip 1 as if to knit, K2 tog, PSSO, YO, K1, YO, K3 tog, YO, K2 tog, YO, ★ K7, YO, SSK, YO, slip 1 as if to knit, K2 tog, PSSO, YO, K1, YO, K3 tog, YO, K2 tog, YO; repeat from ★ around to last 4 sts, K4.

Rnd 79: K4, (YO, SSK) twice, K1, (K2 tog, YO) twice, ★ K9, (YO, SSK) twice, K1, (K2 tog, YO) twice; repeat from ★ around to last 5 sts, K5.

Rnd 81: ★ K2 tog, K3, YO, SSK, YO, slip 1 as if to knit, K2 tog, PSSO, YO, K2 tog, YO, K3, SSK, YO, K1, YO; repeat from ★ around.

Rnd 83: ★ K5, YO, SSK, YO, slip 1 as if to knit, K2 tog, PSSO, YO, K5, YO, slip 2 tog as if to knit, K1, P2SSO, YO; repeat from ★ around.

Rnd 85: Remove marker, K1, place marker, ★ K5, YO, slip 1 as if to knit, K2 tog, PSSO, YO, K5, SSK, YO, K1, YO, K2 tog; repeat from ★ around.

Rnd 87: K5, slip 2 tog as if to knit, K1, P2SSO, ★ K 15, slip 2 tog as if to knit, K1, P2SSO; repeat from ★ around to last 10 sts, K 10: 160 sts.

Rnd 89: Knit around to last 2 sts, slip last 2 sts onto right needle tip and remove marker, slip same 2 sts back onto left needle tip and place marker.

Rnds 90-96: Knit around.

Rnd 97: ★ YO, SSK, K 11, K2 tog, YO, K1 tbl; repeat from ★ around.

Rnd 98 AND ALL EVEN-NUMBERED RNDS THRU Rnd 114: Knit around.

Rnd 99: ★ K1 tbl, YO, SSK, K9, (K2 tog, YO) twice; repeat from ★ around.

Rnd 101: ★ (YO, SSK) twice, K1, SSK, YO, K1, YO, K2 tog, K1, (K2 tog, YO) twice, K1; repeat from ★ around.

Rnd 103: K1, (YO, SSK) twice, K1, YO, slip 2 tog as if to knit, K1, P2SSO, YO, K1, (K2 tog, YO) twice, ★ K3, (YO, SSK) twice, K1, YO, slip 2 tog as if to knit, K1, P2SSO, YO, K1, (K2 tog, YO) twice; repeat from ★ around to last 2 sts, K2.

Rnd 105: K2, YO, SSK, YO, slip 1 as if to knit, K2 tog, PSSO, YO, K1, YO, K3 tog, YO, K2 tog, YO, ★ K5, YO, SSK, YO, slip 1 as if to knit, K2 tog, PSSO, YO, K1, YO, K3 tog, YO, K2 tog, YO; repeat from ★ around to last 3 sts, K3.

Rnd 107: K3, (YO, SSK) twice, K1, (K2 tog, YO) twice, ★ K7, (YO, SSK) twice, K1, (K2 tog, YO) twice; repeat from ★ around to last 4 sts, K4.

Rnd 109: ★ K2 tog, K2, YO, SSK, YO, slip 1 as if to knit, K2 tog, PSSO, YO, K2 tog, YO, K2, SSK, YO, K1, YO; repeat from ★ around.

Rnd 111: ★ K4, YO, SSK, YO, slip 1 as if to knit, K2 tog, PSSO, YO, K4, YO, slip 2 tog as if to knit, K1, P2SSO, YO; repeat from ★ around.

Rnd 113: Remove marker, K1, place marker, ★ K4, YO, slip 1 as if to knit, K2 tog, PSSO, YO, K4, SSK, YO, K1, YO, K2 tog; repeat from ★ around.

Rnd 115: K4, slip 2 tog as if to knit, K1, P2SSO, ★ K 13, slip 2 tog as if to knit, K1, P2SSO; repeat from ★ around to last 9 sts, K9: 140 sts.

Rnds 116-122: Knit around.

Rnd 123: Knit around decreasing 28 sts evenly spaced across to last 2 sts, slip last 2 sts onto right needle tip, remove marker, slip same 2 sts back onto left needle tip, place marker: 112 sts.

BODICE

Change to 16" (40.5 cm) circular knitting needle when there are too few stitches to use a 24" (61 cm) circular knitting needle.

Rnds 1-11: Work same as Rnds 1-11 of Skirt Band, page 2.

Begin working in rows.

Row 1: Remove marker, K2, place marker, **turn**; purl across to marker, remove marker.

Row 2 (Right side)**:** Add on 5 sts (button band), K 11, WYF slip next 5 sts, (K5, WYF slip next 5 sts) across to last 11 sts, K 11: 117 sts.

Row 3: K5, purl across to last 5 sts, K5.

Row 4: K 11, WYF slip next 5 sts, (K5, WYF slip next 5 sts) across to last 11 sts, K 11.

Row 5: K5, purl across to last 5 sts, K5.

Row 6: K 11, WYF slip next 5 sts, (K5, WYF slip next 5 sts) across to last 11 sts, K8, [YO, K2 tog (buttonhole made)], K1.

Row 7: K5, P8, ★ † insert right needle under all 3 loose strands from **bottom** to **top** and purl them as one st, P1, with left needle, bring second st on right needle over first st and off needle †, P9; repeat from ★ 8 times **more**, then repeat from † to † once, P8, K5.

Row 8 (Dividing row): [K6, WYF slip next 5 sts, K5, WYF slip next 5 sts, K5 (Left Back)], bind off next 8 sts, [K1, WYF slip next 5 sts, (K5, WYF slip next 5 sts) 4 times, K2 (Front)], bind off next 8 sts, [K4, WYF slip next 5 sts, K5, WYF slip next 5 sts, K6 (Right Back)].

RIGHT BACK
Row 1: With straight knitting needles, K5 (buttonhole band), P 21, slip a point protector on each end of circular knitting needle to keep sts from unraveling while working Right Back: 26 sts.

Row 2: SSK, K3, WYF slip next 5 sts, K5, WYF slip next 5 sts, K6: 25 sts.

Row 3: K5, purl across.

Row 4: SSK, K2, WYF slip next 5 sts, K5, WYF slip next 5 sts, K6: 24 sts.

Row 5: K5, P3, † insert right needle under all 3 loose strands from **bottom** to **top** and purl them as one st, P1, with left needle, bring second st on right needle over first st and off needle †, P9, repeat from † to † once, P5.

Row 6: SSK, K6, WYF slip next 5 sts, K 11: 23 sts.

Row 7: K5, purl across.

Row 8 (Buttonhole row): K7, WYF slip next 5 sts, K8, [YO, K2 tog (**buttonhole made**)], K1.

Row 9: K5, purl across.

Row 10: K7, WYF slip next 5 sts, K 11.

Row 11: K5, P8, insert right needle under all 3 loose strands from **bottom** to **top** and purl them as one st, P1, with left needle, bring second st on right needle over first st and off needle, P9.

Row 12: K2, WYF slip next 5 sts, K5, WYF slip next 5 sts, K6.

Row 13: K5, purl across.

Rows 14-16: Repeat Rows 12 and 13 once, then repeat Row 12 once **more**.

Row 17: K5, P3, † insert right needle under all 3 loose strands from **bottom** to **top** and purl them as one st, P1, with left needle, bring second st on right needle over first st and off needle †, P9, repeat from † to † once, P4.

Rows 18-20: Repeat Rows 8-10.

Rows 21-27: Repeat Rows 9-15.

Row 28: Repeat Row 8.

Row 29: Repeat Row 17.

Bind off all sts in **knit**.

FRONT

Row 1: With **wrong** side facing and using straight knitting needles, purl 49 sts from circular knitting needle, slip a point protector on each end of circular knitting needle to keep sts from unraveling while working Front: 49 sts.

Row 2: SSK, WYF slip next 5 sts, (K5, WYF slip next 5 sts) 4 times, K2 tog: 47 sts.

Row 3: Purl across.

Row 4: SSK, WYF slip next 4 sts, K5, (WYF slip next 5 sts, K5) 3 times, WYF slip next 4 sts, K2 tog: 45 sts.

Row 5: P2, ★ † insert right needle under all 3 loose strands from **bottom** to **top** and purl them as one st, P1, with left needle, bring second st on right needle over first st and off needle †, P9; repeat from ★ 3 times **more**, then repeat from † to † once, P2.

Row 6: SSK, K3, WYF slip next 5 sts, (K5, WYF slip next 5 sts) 3 times, K3, K2 tog: 43 sts.

Row 7: Purl across.

Row 8: K4, WYF slip next 5 sts, (K5, WYF slip next 5 sts) 3 times, K4.

Rows 9 and 10: Repeat Rows 7 and 8.

Row 11: P6, ★ † insert right needle under all 3 loose strands from **bottom** to **top** and purl them as one st, P1, with left needle, bring second st on right needle over first st and off needle †, P9; repeat from ★ 2 times **more**, then repeat from † to † once, P6.

Row 12: K9, WYF slip next 5 sts, (K5, WYF slip next 5 sts) twice, K9.

Row 13: Purl across.

Rows 14-16: Repeat Rows 12 and 13 once, then repeat Row 12 once **more**.

Row 17: P 11, ★ † insert right needle under all 3 loose strands from **bottom** to **top** and purl them as one st, P1, with left needle, bring second st on right needle over first st and off needle †, P9; repeat from ★ once **more**, then repeat from † to † once, P 11.

Row 18: Repeat Row 8.

Rows 19-23: Repeat Rows 7-11.

NECK SHAPING

Row 1: K9, WYF slip next 5 sts, K3, bind off next 9 sts, K2, WYF slip next 5 sts, knit across: 17 sts **each** side.

Both sides of Neck are worked at the same time, using separate yarn for each side.

Row 2: Purl across to within 2 sts of Neck edge, P2 tog; with second yarn, P2 tog tbl, purl across: 16 sts **each** side.

Row 3: K9, WYF slip next 5 sts, K2 tog; with second yarn, SSK, WYF slip next 5 sts, knit across: 15 sts **each** side.

Row 4: Purl across to within 2 sts of Neck edge, P2 tog; with second yarn, P2 tog tbl, purl across: 14 sts **each** side.

Row 5: K9, WYF slip next 4 sts, K1; with second yarn, K1, WYF slip next 4 sts, knit across.

Row 6: P 11, † insert right needle under all 3 loose strands from **bottom** to **top** and purl them as one st, P1, with left needle, bring second st on right needle over first st and off needle †, P2 tog; with second yarn, P2 tog tbl, repeat from † to † once, P 11: 13 sts **each** side.

Row 7: Bind off remaining sts on first side in **knit**, leaving a long end for sewing; with second yarn, knit across.

Bind off remaining sts in **purl**, leaving a long end for sewing.

LEFT BACK
Row 1: With **wrong** side facing and using straight knitting needles, P 21 from circular knitting needle, K5 (button band): 26 sts.

Row 2: K6, WYF slip next 5 sts, K5, WYF slip next 5 sts, K3, K2 tog: 25 sts.

Row 3: Purl across to last 5 sts, K5.

Row 4: K6, WYF slip next 5 sts, K5, WYF slip next 5 sts, K2, K2 tog: 24 sts.

Row 5: P5, † insert right needle under all 3 loose strands from **bottom** to **top** and purl them as one st, P1, with left needle, bring second st on right needle over first st and off needle †, P9, repeat from † to † once, P3, K5.

Row 6: K 11, WYF slip next 5 sts, K6, K2 tog: 23 sts.

Row 7: Purl across to last 5 sts, K5.

Row 8: K 11, WYF slip next 5 sts, K7.

Rows 9 and 10: Repeat Rows 7 and 8.

Row 11: P9, insert right needle under all 3 loose strands from **bottom** to **top** and purl them as one st, P1, with left needle, bring second st on right needle over first st and off needle, P8, K5.

Row 12: K6, WYF slip next 5 sts, K5, WYF slip next 5 sts, K2.

Row 13: Purl across to last 5 sts, K5.

Rows 14-16: Repeat Rows 12 and 13 once, then repeat Row 12 once **more**.

Row 17: P4, † insert right needle under all 3 loose strands from **bottom** to **top** and purl them as one st, P1, with left needle, bring second st on right needle over first st and off needle †, P9, repeat from † to † once, P3, K5.

Row 18: K 11, WYF slip next 5 sts, K7.

Row 19: Purl across to last 5 sts, K5.

Rows 20-22: Repeat Rows 18 and 19 once, then repeat Row 18 once **more**.

Rows 23-29: Repeat Rows 11-17.

Bind off all sts in **knit**.

Sew shoulder seams.

SLEEVE (Make 2)

BAND
With straight knitting needles, cast on 25 sts.

Row 1: P1, (WYF slip 1, P1) across.

Row 2: P1, (K1, P1) across.

Row 3: Knit across.

Row 4: Purl across.

Rows 5-8: Repeat Rows 1-4.

BODY

Row 1: Knit increase in each st across: 50 sts.

Row 2: Purl across.

Row 3: K2, WYF slip next 5 sts, (K5, WYF slip next 5 sts) 4 times, K3.

Rows 4-7: Repeat Rows 2 and 3 twice.

Row 8: P5, ★ † insert right needle under all 3 loose strands from **bottom** to **top** and purl them as one st, P1, with left needle, bring second st on right needle over first st and off needle †, P9; repeat from ★ 3 times **more**, then repeat from † to † once, P4.

Row 9: K7, WYF slip next 5 sts, (K5, WYF slip next 5 sts) 3 times, K8.

Row 10: Purl across.

Cap Shaping

Row 1: Bind off 4 sts, K2, WYF slip next 5 sts, (K5, WYF slip next 5 sts) 3 times, K8: 46 sts.

Row 2: Bind off 4 sts, purl across: 42 sts.

Row 3: SSK, K1, WYF slip next 5 sts, (K5, WYF slip next 5 sts) 3 times, K2, K2 tog: 40 sts.

Row 4: P5, ★ † insert right needle under all 3 loose strands from **bottom** to **top** and purl them as one st, P1, with left needle, bring second st on right needle over first st and off needle †, P9; repeat from ★ 2 times **more**, then repeat from † to † once, P4.

Row 5: K7, WYF slip next 5 sts, (K5, WYF slip next 5 sts) twice, K8.

Row 6: Purl across.

Rows 7-9: Repeat Rows 5 and 6 once, then repeat Row 5 once **more**.

Row 10: P 10, ★ † insert right needle under all 3 loose strands from **bottom** to **top**, purl them as one st, P1, with left needle, bring second st on right needle over first st and off needle †, P9; repeat from ★ once **more**, then repeat from † to † once, P9.

Row 11: K2, WYF slip next 5 sts, (K5, WYF slip next 5 sts) 3 times, K3.

Row 12: Purl across.

Rows 13-15: Repeat Rows 11 and 12 once, then repeat Row 11 once **more**.

Row 16: P5, ★ † insert right needle under all 3 loose strands from **bottom** to **top** and purl them as one st, P1, with left needle, bring second st on right needle over first st and off needle †, P9; repeat from ★ 2 times **more**, then repeat from † to † once, P4.

Rows 17-22: Repeat Rows 5-10.

Row 23: K2 tog across: 20 sts.

Row 24: P2 tog across: 10 sts.

Bind off remaining sts in **knit**.

Placing center of last row on Sleeve Cap at shoulder seam and matching bound off sts at underarm, sew Sleeves to Gown.

Weave underarm seam (**Fig. 19**, *page* 39).

Lapping buttonhole band over button band, sew bottom of bands in place.

Sew buttons to button band opposite buttonholes.

BONNET
FRONT BAND
With straight knitting needles, cast on 61 sts.

Row 1: P1, (WYF slip 1, P1) across.

Row 2: P1, (K1, P1) across.

Row 3: Knit across.

Row 4: Purl across.

Rows 5-11: Repeat Rows 1-4 once, then repeat Rows 1-3 once **more**.

Row 12: Purl across decreasing 7 sts evenly spaced: 54 sts.

CROWN
Row 1: K3, ★ YO, SSK, K 11, K2 tog, YO, K1 tbl; repeat from ★ 2 times **more**, K3.

Row 2 AND ALL EVEN-NUMBERED ROWS: Purl across.

Row 3: K3, ★ K1 tbl, YO, SSK, K9, (K2 tog, YO) twice; repeat from ★ 2 times **more**, K3.

Row 5: K3, (YO, SSK) twice, K1, SSK, YO, K1, YO, K2 tog, K1, (K2 tog, YO) twice, ★ K1, (YO, SSK) twice, K1, SSK, YO, K1, YO, K2 tog, K1, (K2 tog, YO) twice; repeat from ★ once **more**, K4.

Row 7: K4, (YO, SSK) twice, K1, YO, slip 2 tog as if to **knit**, K1, P2SSO, YO, K1, (K2 tog, YO) twice, ★ K3, (YO, SSK) twice, K1, YO, slip 2 tog as if to **knit**, K1, P2SSO, YO, K1, (K2 tog, YO) twice; repeat from ★ once **more**, K5.

Row 9: ★ K5, YO, SSK, YO, slip 1 as if to **knit**, K2 tog, PSSO, YO, K1, YO, K3 tog, YO, K2 tog, YO; repeat from ★ 2 times **more**, K6.

Row 11: K6, ★ (YO, SSK) twice, K1, (K2 tog, YO) twice, K7; repeat from ★ across.

Rnd 13: K7, YO, SSK, YO, slip 1 as if to knit, K2 tog, PSSO, YO, K2 tog, YO, ★ K2, SSK, YO, K1, YO, K2 tog, K2, YO, SSK, YO, slip 1 as if to knit, K2 tog, PSSO, YO, K2 tog, YO; repeat from ★ once more, K8.

Rnd 15: K8, YO, SSK, YO, slip 1 as if to knit, K2 tog, PSSO, YO, ★ K4, YO, slip 2 tog as if to knit, K1, P2SSO, YO, K4, YO, SSK, YO, slip 1 as if to knit, K2 tog, PSSO, YO; repeat from ★ once more, K9.

Row 17: K9, YO, slip 1 as if to knit, K2 tog, PSSO, YO, ★ K4, SSK, YO, K1, YO, K2 tog, K4, YO, slip 1 as if to knit, K2 tog, PSSO, YO; repeat from ★ once more, K 10.

Beginning with a **purl** row, work in Stockinette Stitch until piece measures approximately 4" (10 cm) from cast on edge, ending by working a **purl** row.

SHAPING
Row 1: (K7, K2 tog) across: 48 sts.

Row 2 AND ALL EVEN-NUMBERED ROWS: Knit across.

Row 3: (K6, K2 tog) across: 42 sts.

Row 5: (K5, K2 tog) across: 36 sts.

Row 7: (K4, K2 tog) across: 30 sts.

Row 9: (K3, K2 tog) across: 24 sts.

Row 11: (K2, K2 tog) across: 18 sts.

Row 13: (K1, K2 tog) across: 12 sts.

Row 15: K2 tog across: 6 sts.

Cut yarn, leaving a long end for sewing.

Thread tapestry needle with long end and weave needle through remaining sts on Row 15; gather tightly and secure end. With same end, sew ends of rows on Shaping together.

NECK BAND
With **right** side facing and using straight knitting needles, pick up 45 sts evenly spaced across neck edge (**Fig. 18, page 39**).

Rows 1 and 2: Knit across.

Row 3 (Eyelet row)**:** P1, (YO, P2 tog) across.

Rows 4 and 5: Knit across.

Bind off all sts in **knit**.

Weave ribbon through Eyelet row for ties.

BOOTIES
SOLE
With straight knitting needles, cast on 19 sts.

Row 1 (Right side)**:** K9, place marker, K1, place marker, K9.

Rows 2-6: K1, knit increase, knit across to within one st of first marker, knit increase, slip marker, K1, slip marker, knit increase, knit across to last 2 sts, knit increase, K1: 39 sts.

Rows 7-14: Knit across removing markers on Row 7.

INSTEP
Row 1: K 24, turn; leave remaining 15 sts unworked.

Row 2: Slip 1 as if to purl, P7, P2 tog, turn.

Row 3: Slip 1 as if to purl, K7, SSK, turn.

Row 4: Slip 1 as if to purl, P7, P2 tog, turn.

Row 5: Slip 1 as if to purl, K1, WYF slip next 5 sts, K1, SSK, turn.

Rows 6-9: Repeat Rows 4 and 5 twice.

Row 10: Slip 1 as if to purl, P3, insert right needle under all 3 loose strands from **bottom** to **top**, purl them as one st, P1, with left needle, bring second st on right needle over first st and off needle, P3, P2 tog, **turn.**

Row 11: Slip 1 as if to purl, K7, K2 tog tbl, **turn.**

Row 12: Slip 1 as if to purl, P7, P2 tog, **turn.**

Row 13: Slip 1 as if to purl, K7, K2 tog tbl, knit across: 27 sts.

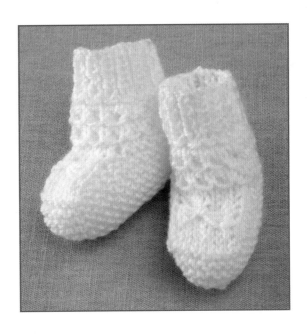

CUFF
Row 1: Purl across.

Row 2 (Right side): P1, (WYF slip 1, P1) across.

Row 3: P1, (K1, P1) across.

Row 4: Knit across.

Rows 5-10: Repeat Rows 1-4 once, then repeat Rows 1 and 2 once **more.**

Row 11: K1, (P1, K1) across.

Row 12: P1, (K1, P1) across.

Rows 13-16: Repeat Rows 11 and 12 twice.

Bind off all sts in ribbing, leaving a long end for sewing.

Sew back and Sole in one continuous seam.

Size: Newborn to 3 months

MATERIALS

Light Weight Yarn ◖**3**◗

[7 ounces, 575 yards
(198 grams, 525 meters) per skein]:
  2 skeins
Straight knitting needles, size 6 (4 mm) **or** size
  needed for gauge
16" (40.5 cm) Circular knitting needle,
  size 6 (4 mm)
Crochet hook, size D (3.25 mm) (for Trim)
Stitch holder
Markers
$^9/_{16}$" (14 mm) Buttons - 3
$^1/_4$" (7 mm) wide Ribbon - 48" (122 cm)
$^1/_8$" (3 mm) wide Ribbon - 76" (193 cm)
Sewing needle and matching thread
Tapestry needle

GAUGE: In Stockinette Stitch,
     22 sts and 28 rows = 4" (10 cm)

Techniques used:

- YO (Figs. 4a, c, & d, page 36)
- Knit increase (Figs. 5a & b, page 36)
- K2 tog (Fig. 9, page 37)
- P2 tog (Fig. 12, page 38)
- P2 tog tbl (Fig. 13, page 38)
- SSK (Figs. 15a-c, page 38)
- P3 tog (Fig. 14, page 38)
- Basic Crochet Stitches (Figs. 20-23, page 40)

GOWN
FRONT BODICE

With straight knitting needles, cast on 55 sts.

Rows 1 and 2: Knit across.

Row 3: K3, YO, K2 tog, (K6, YO, K2 tog) across to last 2 sts, K2.

Row 4 (Right side): Purl across.

Row 5: Knit across.

Rows 6 and 7: Repeat Rows 4 and 5.

Row 8: P3, ★ † insert right needle from **bottom** to **top** under strands below **and** above YO 5 rows below and place both strands onto needle, insert left needle from **front** to **back** through first 2 sts on right needle and slip them onto left needle, then purl these 2 sts tog as if they were one st, P2 tog †, P6; repeat from ★ 5 times **more**, then repeat from † to † once, P2.

Row 9: K7, YO, K2 tog, (K6, YO, K2 tog) across to last 6 sts, K6.

Armhole Shaping

Row 1: Bind off 3 sts, purl across: 52 sts.

Row 2: Bind off 3 sts, knit across: 49 sts.

Row 3 (Decrease row): P2 tog, purl across to last 2 sts, P2 tog tbl: 47 sts.

Row 4: Knit across.

Front

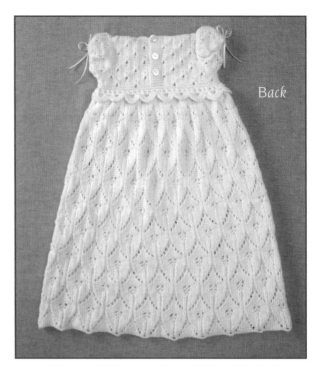
Back

Row 5: P2 tog, P1, ★ † insert right needle from bottom to top under strands below and above YO 5 rows below and place both strands onto needle, insert left needle from front to back through first 2 sts on right needle and slip them onto left needle, then purl these 2 sts tog as if they were one st, P2 tog †, P6; repeat from ★ 4 times more, then repeat from † to † once, P2 tog tbl: 45 sts.

Row 6: (K6, YO, K2 tog) across to last 5 sts, K5.

Rows 7-10: Repeat Rows 3 and 4 twice: 41 sts.

Row 11: P4, ★ † insert right needle from bottom to top under strands below and above YO 5 rows below and place both strands onto needle, insert left needle from front to back through first 2 sts on right needle and slip them onto left needle, then purl these 2 sts tog as if they were one st, P2 tog †, P6; repeat from ★ 3 times more, then repeat from † to † once, P3.

Row 12: K8, YO, K2 tog, (K6, YO, K2 tog) 3 times, K7.

Row 13: Purl across.

Row 14: Knit across.

Rows 15 and 16: Repeat Rows 13 and 14.

Row 17: P8, ★ † insert right needle from bottom to top under strands below and above YO 5 rows below and place both strands onto needle, insert left needle from front to back through first 2 sts on right needle and slip them onto left needle, then purl these 2 sts tog as if they were one st, P2 tog †, P6; repeat from ★ 2 times more, then repeat from † to † once, P7.

Row 18: K4, YO, K2 tog, (K6, YO, K2 tog) across to last 3 sts, K3.

Rows 19-22: Repeat Rows 13-16.

Row 23: Repeat Row 11.

Neck Shaping
Row 1: K8, YO, K2 tog, K5, bind off next 11 sts, K5, YO, K2 tog, K7: 15 sts **each** side.

Both sides of Neck are worked at the same time, using separate yarn for **each** side.

Row 2 (Decrease row): Purl across to within 2 sts of Neck edge, P2 tog; with second yarn, P2 tog tbl, purl across: 14 sts **each** side.

Row 3: Knit across; with second yarn, knit across.

Rows 4 and 5: Repeat Rows 2 and 3: 13 sts **each** side.

Row 6: P8, insert right needle from **bottom** to **top** under strands below **and** above YO 5 rows below and place both strands onto needle, insert left needle from **front** to **back** through first 2 sts on right needle and slip them onto left needle, then purl these 2 sts tog as if they were one st, P2 tog, P3; with second yarn, P4, insert right needle from **bottom** to **top** under strands below **and** above YO 5 rows below and place both strands onto needle, insert left needle from **front** to **back** through first 2 sts on right needle and slip them onto left needle, then purl these 2 sts tog as if they were one st, P2 tog, P7.

Row 7: Bind off remaining sts on first side in knit, leaving a long end for sewing; with second yarn, knit across.

Bind off remaining sts in **purl**, leaving a long end for sewing.

BACK BODICE
With straight knitting needles, cast on 55 sts.

Rows 1 and 2: Knit across.

Left Back
Row 1: K3, YO, K2 tog, (K6, YO, K2 tog) twice, K9, slip remaining 25 sts onto st holder: 30 sts.

Row 2 (Right side): K5 (button band), purl across.

Row 3: Knit across.

Rows 4 and 5: Repeat Rows 2 and 3.

Row 6: K5, P5, ★ † insert right needle from **bottom** to **top** under strands below **and** above YO 5 rows below and place both strands onto needle, insert left needle from **front** to **back** through first 2 sts on right needle and slip them onto left needle, then purl these 2 sts tog as if they were one st, P2 tog †, P6; repeat from ★ once **more**, then repeat from † to † once, P2.

Row 7: K7, YO, K2 tog, (K6, YO, K2 tog) twice, K5.

Row 8: K5, purl across.

Armhole Shaping
Row 1: Bind off 3 sts, knit across: 27 sts.

Row 2: K5, purl across to last 2 sts, P2 tog tbl: 26 sts.

Row 3: Knit across.

Row 4: K5, P1, ★ † insert right needle from **bottom** to **top** under strands below **and** above YO 5 rows below and place both strands onto needle, insert left needle from **front** to **back** through first 2 sts on right needle and slip them onto left needle, then purl these 2 sts tog as if they were one st, P2 tog †, P6; repeat from ★ once **more**, then repeat from † to † once, P2 tog tbl: 25 sts.

Row 5: (K6, YO, K2 tog) twice, K9.

Row 6 (Decrease row): K5, purl across to last 2 sts, P2 tog tbl: 24 sts.

Row 7: Knit across.

Rows 8 and 9: Repeat Rows 6 and 7: 23 sts.

Row 10: K5, P5, † insert right needle from **bottom** to **top** under strands below **and** above YO 5 rows below and place both strands onto needle, insert left needle from **front** to **back** through first 2 sts on right needle and slip them onto left needle, then purl these 2 sts tog as if they were one st, P2 tog †, P6, repeat from † to † once, P3.

Row 11: K8, YO, K2 tog, K6, YO, K2 tog, K5.

Row 12: K5, purl across.

Row 13: Knit across.

Rows 14 and 15: Repeat Rows 12 and 13.

Row 16: K5, P1, † insert right needle from **bottom** to **top** under strands below **and** above YO 5 rows below and place both strands onto needle, insert left needle from **front** to **back** through first 2 sts on right needle and slip them onto left needle, then purl these 2 sts tog as if they were one st, P2 tog †, P6, repeat from † to † once, P7.

Row 17: K4, YO, K2 tog, K6, YO, K2 tog, K9.

Row 18: K5, purl across.

Row 19-28: Repeat Rows 7-16.

Bind off all sts in **knit**.

Right Back
Row 1: With **wrong** side facing, pick up 5 sts along base of button band (**Fig. 18***b***, page** 39), slip sts from st holder onto empty needle, K5, YO, K2 tog, (K6, YO, K2 tog) twice, K2: 30 sts.

Row 2: Purl across to last 5 sts, K5.

Row 3: Knit across.

Rows 4 and 5: Repeat Rows 2 and 3.

Row 6: P3, ★ † insert right needle from **bottom** to **top** under strands below **and** above YO 5 rows below and place both strands onto needle, insert left needle from **front** to **back** through first 2 sts on right needle and slip them onto left needle, then purl these 2 sts tog as if they were one st, P2 tog †, P6; repeat from ★ once **more**, then repeat from † to † once, P4, K5.

Row 7: K6, (YO, K2 tog, K6) across.

Armhole Shaping
Row 1: Bind off 3 sts, purl across to last 5 sts, K5: 27 sts.

Row 2: Knit across.

Row 3 (Buttonhole row)**:** P2 tog, purl across to last 5 sts, K2, [YO, K2 tog (buttonhole made)], K1: 26 sts.

Row 4: Knit across.

Row 5: P2 tog, P1, ★ † insert right needle from **bottom** to **top** under strands below **and** above YO 5 rows below and place both strands onto needle, insert left needle from **front** to **back** through first 2 sts on right needle and slip them onto left needle, then purl these 2 sts tog as if they were one st, P2 tog †, P6; repeat from ★ once **more**, then repeat from † to † once, K5: 25 sts.

Row 6: K 10, YO, K2 tog, K6, YO, K2 tog, K5.

Row 7 (Decrease row)**:** P2 tog, purl across to last 5 sts, K5: 24 sts.

Row 8: Knit across.

Rows 9 and 10: Repeat Rows 7 and 8: 23 sts.

Row 11: P4, † insert right needle from **bottom** to **top** under strands below **and** above YO 5 rows below and place both strands onto needle, insert left needle from **front** to **back** through first 2 sts on right needle and slip them onto left needle, then purl these 2 sts tog as if they were one st, P2 tog †, P6, repeat from † to † once, P4, K5.

Row 12: (K6, YO, K2 tog) twice, K7.

Row 13: Purl across to last 5 sts. K5.

Row 14: Knit across.

Row 15 (Buttonhole row)**:** Purl across to last 5 sts, K2, [YO, K2 tog (buttonhole made)], K1.

Row 16: Knit across.

Row 17: P8, † insert right needle from **bottom** to **top** under strands below **and** above YO 5 rows below and place both strands onto needle, insert left needle from **front** to **back** through first 2 sts on right needle and slip them onto left needle, then purl these 2 sts tog as if they were one st, P2 tog †, P6, repeat from † to † once, K5.

Row 18: K 10, YO, K2 tog, K6, YO, K2 tog, K3.

Rows 19-22: Repeat Rows 13 and 14 twice.

Rows 23-29: Repeat Rows 11-17.

Bind off all sts in **knit.**

Sew shoulder seams.

Weave side seams (**Fig.** 19, *page* 39).

SKIRT
With **right** side facing, using circular knitting needle and beginning at center Back, pick up 110 sts around cast on edges of Back and Front Bodice, place marker to mark beginning of rnd (*see Markers, page 35*).

Rnd 1: Purl around.

Rnd 2 (Eyelet rnd)**:** (K2 tog, YO) around.

Rnd 3: ★ K2, knit increase in each of next 53 sts; repeat from ★ once **more**: 216 sts.

Rnd 4: ★ SSK, K3, YO, P1, YO, K3, K2 tog, P1; repeat from ★ around.

Rnd 5: (K5, P1) around.

Rnds 6-9: Repeat Rnds 4 and 5 twice.

Rnd 10: ★ YO, K3, K2 tog, P1, SSK, K3, YO, P1; repeat from ★ around.

Rnd 11: (K5, P1) around.

Rnd 12: P1, YO, K2, K2 tog, P1, SSK, K2, YO, ★ P3, YO, K2, K2 tog, P1, SSK, K2, YO; repeat from ★ around to last 2 sts, P2.

Rnd 13: (P1, K4) twice, (P3, K4, P1, K4) around to last 2 sts, P2.

Rnd 14: P2, YO, K1, K2 tog, P1, SSK, K1, YO, ★ P5, YO, K1, K2 tog, P1, SSK, K1, YO; repeat from ★ around to last 3 sts, P3.

Rnd 15: P2, K3, P1, K3, (P5, K3, P1, K3) around to last 3 sts, P3.

Rnd 16: P3, YO, K2 tog, P1, SSK, YO, ★ P7, YO, K2 tog, P1, SSK, YO; repeat from ★ around to last 4 sts, P4.

Rnd 17: P3, K2, P1, K2, (P7, K2, P1, K2) around to last 4 sts, P4.

Rnds 18-23: Repeat Rnds 10 and 11, 3 times.

Rnd 24: ★ SSK, K3, YO, P1, YO, K3, K2 tog, P1; repeat from ★ around.

Rnd 25: (K5, P1) around.

Rnd 26: ★ SSK, K2, YO, P3, YO, K2, K2 tog, P1; repeat from ★ around.

Rnd 27: (K4, P3, K4, P1) around.

Rnd 28: ★ SSK, K1, YO, P5, YO, K1, K2 tog, P1; repeat from ★ around.

Rnd 29: (K3, P5, K3, P1) around.

Rnd 30: ★ SSK, YO, P7, YO, K2 tog, P1; repeat from ★ around.

Rnd 31: (K2, P7, K2, P1) around.

Rnds 32-129: Repeat Rnds 4-31, 3 times; then repeat Rnds 4-17 once **more.**

Bind Off Rnd: Bind off 4 sts, [(slip st back onto left needle and knit the st) 4 times (Picot made)], K2 tog, slip second st on right needle over first st, ★ bind off 10 sts, work Picot, K2 tog, slip second st on right needle over first st; repeat from ★ around to last 5 sts, bind off remaining sts.

TRIM
Rnd 1: Hold Gown with **right** side facing and Bodice toward you. With crochet hook and working in purl bumps on Rnd 1 of Skirt, join yarn with slip st in center st of Back; ch 3 **(counts as first dc)**, skip next st, dc in next st, ★ ch 1, skip next st, dc in next st; repeat from ★ around to last st, skip last st; join with slip st to first dc: 108 sts total (55 dc and 53 chs).

Rnd 2: Slip st in next 2 sts, ch 5, ★ skip next dc, slip st in next 5 sts, ch 5; repeat from ★ around to last 3 sts, skip next dc, slip st in last 2 sts; join with slip st to joining slip st: 18 ch-5 sps.

Row 3: (5 Dc, ch 2, 5 dc) in next ch-5 sp and in each ch-5 sp around; join with slip st to joining slip st, finish off.

SLEEVE (Make 2)
BODY
With straight knitting needles, cast on 27 sts.

Rows 1 and 2: Knit across.

Row 3 (Eyelet row): K1, (YO, K2 tog) across.

Row 4: K 13, knit increase, knit across: 28 sts.

Row 5 (Right side): Knit increase in each st across to last st, K1: 55 sts.

Row 6: K3, YO, K2 tog, (K6, YO, K2 tog) across to last 2 sts, K2.

Row 7: Purl across.

Row 8: Knit across.

Rows 9 and 10: Repeat Rows 7 and 8.

Row 11: P3, ★ † insert right needle from **bottom** to **top** under strands below **and** above YO 5 rows below and place both strands onto needle, insert left needle from **front** to **back** through first 2 sts on right needle and slip them onto left needle, then purl these 2 sts tog as if they were one st, P2 tog †, P6; repeat from ★ 5 times **more**, then repeat from † to † once, P2.

Row 12: K7, YO, K2 tog, (K6, YO, K2 tog) across to last 6 sts, K6.

CAP SHAPING
Row 1: Bind off 3 sts, purl across: 52 sts.

Row 2: Bind off 3 sts, knit across: 49 sts.

Row 3: P2 tog, purl across to last 2 sts, P2 tog tbl: 47 sts.

Row 4: SSK, knit across to last 2 sts, K2 tog: 45 sts.

Row 5: P2 tog, ★ † insert right needle from **bottom** to **top** under strands below **and** above YO 5 rows below and place both strands onto needle, insert left needle from **front** to **back** through first 2 sts on right needle and slip them onto left needle, then purl these 2 sts tog as if they were one st †, P2 tog, P6; repeat from ★ 4 times **more**, then repeat from † to † once, P3 tog: 43 sts.

Row 6: SSK, K 11, YO, K2 tog, (K6, YO, K2 tog) twice, K 10, K2 tog: 41 sts.

Row 7 (Decrease row): P2 tog, purl across to last 2 sts, P2 tog tbl: 39 sts.

Row 8 (Decrease row): SSK, knit across to last 2 sts, K2 tog: 37 sts.

Rows 9 and 10: Repeat Rows 7 and 8: 33 sts.

Row 11: P2 tog, P6, ★ † insert right needle from **bottom** to **top** under strands below **and** above YO 5 rows below and place both strands onto needle, insert left needle from **front** to **back** through first 2 sts on right needle and slip them onto left needle, then purl these 2 sts tog as if they were one st, P2 tog †, P6; repeat from ★ once **more**, then repeat from † to † once, P5, P2 tog tbl: 31 sts.

Row 12: SSK, K9, YO, K2 tog, K6, YO, K2 tog, K8, K2 tog: 29 sts.

Rows 13-16: Repeat Rows 7-10: 21 sts.

Row 17: P2 tog, P4, † insert right needle from **bottom** to **top** under strands below **and** above YO 5 rows below and place both strands onto needle, insert left needle from **front** to **back** through first 2 sts on right needle and slip them onto left needle, then purl these 2 sts tog as if they were one st, P2 tog †, P6, repeat from † to † once, P3, P2 tog tbl: 19 sts.

Row 18: SSK, knit across to last 2 sts, K2 tog: 17 sts.

Row 19: P2 tog, purl across to last 2 sts, P2 tog tbl: 15 sts.

Bind off remaining sts in **knit**.

Placing center of last row on Sleeve Cap at shoulder seam and matching bound off sts at underarm, sew Sleeves to Gown.

Weave Sleeve seam.

Sew buttons to button band opposite buttonholes.

Cut two 24" (61 cm) lengths of ⅛" (3 mm) ribbon. Using photo as a guide, weave one length through Eyelet row on each Sleeve; tie into a bow.

Cut ¼" (7 mm) length of ribbon in half, wrap one piece of ribbon around center dc on front of Gown; tie into a bow.

BONNET
CROWN
With straight knitting needles, cast on 63 sts.

Rows 1 and 2: Knit across.

Row 3 (Eyelet row): K3, YO, K2 tog, (K6, YO, K2 tog) across to last 2 sts, K2.

Row 4 (Right side): Purl across.

Row 5: Knit across.

Rows 6 and 7: Repeat Rows 4 and 5.

Row 8: P3, ★ † insert right needle from **bottom** to **top** under strands below **and** above YO 5 rows below and place both strands onto needle, insert left needle from **front** to **back** through first 2 sts on right needle and slip them onto left needle, then purl these 2 sts tog as if they were one st, P2 tog †, P6; repeat from ★ 6 times **more**, then repeat from † to † once, P2.

Row 9: K7, (YO, K2 tog, K6) across.

Rows 10-13: Repeat Rows 4-7.

Row 14: P7, ★ insert right needle from **bottom** to **top** under strands below **and** above YO 5 rows below and place both strands onto needle, insert left needle from **front** to **back** through first 2 sts on right needle and slip them onto left needle, then purl these 2 sts tog as if they were one st, P2 tog, P6; repeat from ★ across.

Rows 15-26: Repeat Rows 3-14.

Row 27: Knit across.

SHAPING

Row 1: (K6, K2 tog) across to last 7 sts, K7: 56 sts.

Row 2 and ALL EVEN-NUMBERED ROWS: Knit across.

Row 3: (K5, K2 tog) across: 48 sts.

Row 5: (K4, K2 tog) across: 40 sts.

Row 7: (K3, K2 tog) across: 32 sts.

Row 9: (K2, K2 tog) across: 24 sts.

Row 11: (K1, K2 tog) across: 16 sts.

Row 13: K2 tog across: 8 sts.

Cut yarn, leaving a long end for sewing.

Thread tapestry needle with long end and slip remaining sts on Row 13 onto needle; gather **tightly** and secure end. With same end, sew ends of rows on Shaping together.

TRIM

Row 1: Hold Bonnet with **right** side facing and neck to your right. With crochet hook and working across cast on edge, join yarn with slip st in first st, ch 4 **(counts as first dc plus ch 1)**, skip next 2 sts, dc in next st, ★ ch 1, skip next st, dc in next st; repeat from ★ across to last 3 sts, ch 1, skip next 2 sts, dc in last st: 61 sts total (31 dc and 30 chs).

Row 2: Turn; slip st in first 3 sts, ch 5, ★ skip next ch, slip st in next 5 sts, ch 5; repeat from ★ around to last 4 sts, skip next ch, slip st in last 3 sts: 10 ch-5 sps.

Row 3: Turn; (5 dc, ch 2, 5 dc) in first ch-5 sp and in each ch-5 sp across to last 3 slip sts, skip next 2 slip sts, slip st in last slip st; finish off.

NECK BAND

With **right** side facing, using straight knitting needles, and beginning and ending in Row 1 of Trim, pick up 45 sts evenly spaced across **(Fig. 18a, page 39)**: 45 sts.

Row 1: Knit across.

Row 2 (Eyelet row): K1, (YO, K2 tog) across.

Rows 3 and 4: Knit across.

Bind off all sts in **knit**.

Weave remaining length of ¼" (7 mm) ribbon through Eyelet row for ties.

BOOTIES

SOLE

With straight knitting needles, cast on 19 sts.

Row 1 (Right side)**:** K9, place marker, K1, place marker, K9.

Rows 2-6: K1, knit increase, knit across to within one st of first marker, knit increase, slip marker, K1, slip marker, knit increase, knit across to last 2 sts, knit increase, K1: 39 sts.

Rows 7-14: Knit across removing markers on Row 7.

INSTEP

Row 1: K 24, **turn**; leave remaining 15 sts unworked.

Row 2: Slip 1 as if to **purl**, P7, P2 tog, **turn**.

Row 3: Slip 1 as if to **purl**, K7, SSK, **turn**.

Rows 4-12: Repeat Rows 2 and 3, 4 times; then repeat Row 2 once **more**.

Row 13: Slip 1 as if to **purl**, K7, SSK, knit across: 27 sts.

CUFF

Row 1 (Wrong side)**:** Purl across.

Row 2 (Eyelet row)**:** K1, (YO, K2 tog) across.

Row 3: Purl across.

Row 4: Knit across.

Rows 5-13: Repeat Rows 3 and 4, 4 times; then repeat Row 3 once **more**.

Rows 14-16: Knit across.

Bind off all sts in **knit**, leaving a long end for sewing.

Sew back and Sole in one continuous seam.

TRIM

Rnd 1: Hold Bootie with **right** side facing and Cuff to you. With crochet hook and working in remaining purl bumps on Row 15, join yarn with slip st in first st; ch 4 (**counts as first dc plus ch 1**), (skip next st, dc in next st, ch 1) 11 times, skip last 2 sts; join with slip st to first dc: 24 sts total (12 dc and 12 chs).

Rnd 2: Slip st in next 3 sts, ch 5, ★ skip next dc, slip st in next 5 sts, ch 5; repeat from ★ around to last 2 sts, skip next dc, slip st in last ch; join with slip st to joining slip st: 4 ch-5 sps.

Rnd 3: (5 Dc, ch 2, 5 dc) in first ch-5 sp and in each ch-5 sp across; join with slip st to joining slip st, finish off.

Cut remaining length of ⅛" (3 mm) ribbon in half.

Weave one piece of ribbon through Eyelet row, beginning and ending at center front; then tie into a bow.

Repeat for remaining Bootie.

Bouncing Boy

INTERMEDIATE

Size: Newborn to 3 months

MATERIALS
Light Weight Yarn **3**
[7 ounces, 575 yards
(198 grams, 525 meters) per skein]:
  2 skeins
Straight knitting needles, sizes 3 (3.25 mm) **and**
  6 (4 mm) **or** sizes needed for gauge
16" (40.5 cm) Circular knitting needle,
  size 6 (4 mm)
Double pointed knitting needles, size 6 (4 mm)
  (for pleats only) - 2
Stitch holder
Point protectors
Markers
Snaps - 10
½" (12 mm) Buttons - 4
Sewing needle and matching thread
Tapestry needle

GAUGE: With larger size knitting needles,
        in Stockinette Stitch,
        22 sts and 28 rows = 4" (10 cm)

Techniques used:
- K1 tbl (*Fig. 1, page 35*)
- P1 tbl (*Fig. 2, page 35*)
- Knit increase (*Figs. 5a & b, page 36*)
- Purl increase (*Fig. 6, page 37*)
- YO (*Fig. 4a, page 36*)
- M1 (*Figs. 7a & b, page 37*)
- Adding new sts (*Figs. 8a & b, page 37*)
- K2 tog (*Fig. 9, page 37*)
- K2 tog tbl (*Fig. 10, page 37*)
- SSK (*Figs. 15a-c, page 38*)
- P2 tog (*Fig. 12, page 38*)
- P2 tog tbl (*Fig. 13, page 38*)

ROMPER
FIRST SIDE
RIBBING
With smaller size knitting needles, cast on 35 sts.

Row 1 (Right side): (K1 tbl, P1) across.

Row 2: (K1, P1 tbl) across.

Rows 3-6: Repeat Rows 1 and 2 twice.

Row 7: K1, knit increase in each st across to last st, K1: 68 sts.

LEG
Change to larger size straight knitting needles.

Row 1: Purl across.

Row 2 (Increase row): Knit increase, knit across to last st, knit increase: 70 sts.

Rows 3-6: Repeat Rows 1 and 2 twice: 74 sts.

Row 7: Knit across.

Row 8 (Increase row): Knit increase, knit across to last st, knit increase: 76 sts.

Rows 9 and 10: Repeat Rows 7 and 8: 78 sts.

Row 11: Purl across.

Row 12: Knit increase, K2, (P4, K4) across to last 3 sts, P2, knit increase: 80 sts.

Row 13: K3, P4, (K4, P4) across to last st, K1.

Row 14: Knit increase, P1, K4, (P4, K4) across to last 2 sts, P1, knit increase: 82 sts.

Row 15: K2, (P4, K4) across.

Front

Back

Row 16: Knit increase, K3, P4, (K4, P4) across to last 2 sts, K1, knit increase: 84 sts.

Row 17: P4, (K4, P4) across.

Row 18: Knit increase, K2, (P4, K4) across to last st, knit increase: 86 sts.

Row 19: K3, (P4, K4) across to last 3 sts, P3.

Row 20: Knit increase, knit across to last st, knit increase: 88 sts.

Row 21: Purl across.

Row 22: Purl increase, purl across to last st, purl increase: 90 sts.

Row 23: Purl across.

Row 24: Purl increase, purl across to last st, purl increase: 92 sts.

Rows 25-32: Repeat Rows 1 and 2, 4 times: 100 sts.

Work even until piece measures approximately 6½" (16.5 cm) from cast on edge, ending by working a **purl** row.

Shaping
Rows 1 and 2: Bind off 5 sts, work across: 90 sts.

Cut yarn; slip remaining sts onto st holder.

SECOND SIDE
Work same as First Side; do **not** cut yarn **or** remove sts from needle.

BODY
Rnd 1 (Right side): With circular knitting needle and working across sts on Second Side (sts on straight knitting needle), SSK, knit across to last 2 sts, K2 tog, place marker (*see Markers, page 35*); slip sts from st holder onto opposite tip of circular knitting needle, SSK, knit across to last 2 sts, K2 tog, place marker to mark beginning of rnd: 176 sts.

Rnd 2: Knit around.

Rnd 3: ★ SSK, knit across to within 2 sts of next marker, K2 tog, slip marker; repeat from ★ once more: 172 sts.

Rnd 4: Knit around.

Rnd 5: ★ SSK, knit across to within 2 sts of next marker, K2 tog, slip marker; repeat from ★ once more: 168 sts.

Rnd 6: Knit across to next marker, remove marker, knit across; do **not** remove beginning of rnd marker.

Knit each round until piece measures approximately 14" (35.5 cm) from cast on edge.

Next Rnd (Pleat rnd): ★ † slip next 4 sts onto right needle, slip next 4 sts onto first double pointed needle and turn 180° clockwise, slip next 4 sts onto second double pointed needle, holding both double pointed knitting needles behind left needle, slip 4 sts from right needle back onto left needle (the 3 needles will be parallel), insert right needle as if to **knit** into the first st on left needle, the first st on the second needle, **and** into the first st on the third needle (**Fig. A**), knit these 3 sts tog as if they were one st. [(Knit **next** st on each needle as if they were one st) 3 times (**pleat made**)] †, K1, repeat from † to † once, K 34, ♥ slip next 4 sts onto first double pointed needle, slip next 4 sts onto second double pointed needle and turn 180° counterclockwise, holding both double pointed knitting needles behind left needle (the 3 needles will be parallel), insert right needle as if to **knit** into the first st on left needle, the first st on the second needle, **and** into the first st on the third needle; then knit these 3 sts tog as if they were one st. [(Knit **next** st on each needle as if they were one st) 3 times (**pleat made**)] ♥, K1, repeat from ♥ to ♥ once; then repeat from ★ once more: 104 sts and 4 pleats.

Fig. A

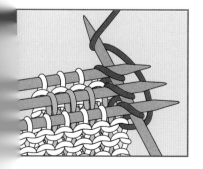

BODICE
Begin working in rows.

Row 1 (Dividing row): M1, K2, **turn**; knit across removing markers, **turn**; add on 5 sts: 110 sts.

Rows 2-4: Knit across.

Row 5: K5, purl across to last 5 sts, K5.

Row 6 (Right side): K5, P4, (K4, P4) across to last 5 sts, K5.

Row 7: K8, (P4, K4) across to last 6 sts, P1, K5.

Row 8 (Buttonhole row): K7, (P4, K4) across to last 7 sts, P2, K2, [YO, K2 tog (**buttonhole made**)], K1.

Row 9: K6, (P4, K4) across to last 8 sts, P3, K5.

Row 10: K5, P3, (K4, P4) across to last 6 sts, K6.

Row 11: K5, P2, (K4, P4) across to last 7 sts, K7.

LEFT BACK
Row 1 (Right side): With larger size straight knitting needles, K5, P1, K4, (P4, K4) twice, leave remaining 84 sts unworked, place a point protector on each end of circular knitting needle to keep the sts from unraveling while working Left Back: 26 sts.

Row 2: K1, P4, (K4, P4) twice, K5 (button band).

Row 3: Knit across to last 2 sts, K2 tog: 25 sts.

Row 4: Purl across to last 5 sts, K5.

Row 5: K5, purl across to last 2 sts, P2 tog: 24 sts.

Row 6: Purl across to last 5 sts, K5.

Row 7: K5, purl across.

Row 8: Purl across to last 5 sts, K5.

Row 9: Knit across.

Row 10: Purl across to last 5 sts, K5.

Rows 11-15: Knit across.

Row 16: Purl across to last 5 sts, K5.

Row 17: K5, (P4, K4) twice, P3.

Row 18: K2, (P4, K4) twice, P1, K5.

Row 19: K7, (P4, K4) twice, P1.

Row 20: (P4, K4) twice, P3, K5.

Row 21: K5, P3, (K4, P4) twice.

Row 22: P1, (K4, P4) twice, K7.

Row 23: K5, P1, (K4, P4) twice, K2.

Row 24: P3, (K4, P4) twice, K5.

Row 25: Knit across.

Row 26: Purl across to last 5 sts, K5.

Row 27: K5, purl across.

Row 28: Purl across to last 5 sts, K5.

Row 29: Bind off 9 sts, P6, **turn**; P7.

Bind off all sts in **knit**.

FRONT
Row 1: With **right** side of sts on circular knitting needle facing and using larger size straight knitting needles, bind off 6 sts, K1, P4, (K4, P4) 5 times, leave remaining 32 sts unworked, place a point protector on each end of circular knitting needle to keep the sts from unraveling while working Front: 46 sts.

Row 2: P1, K4, (P4, K4) across to last st, P1.

Row 3: SSK, knit across to last 2 sts, K2 tog: 44 sts.

Rows 4: Purl across.

Row 5: P2 tog tbl, purl across to last 2 sts, P2 tog: 42 sts.

Rows 6-8: Purl across.

Row 9: Knit across.

Row 10: Purl across.

Rows 11-15: Knit across.

Row 16: Purl across.

Row 17: K3, P4, (K4, P4) across to last 3 sts, K3.

Row 18: P2, (K4, P4) across.

Row 19: P1, (K4, P4) across to last st, K1.

Row 20: (K4, P4) across to last 2 sts, K2.

Neck Shaping
Row 1: K2, P4, K4, P4, K3, bind off next 8 sts, (P4, K4) twice: 17 sts **each** side.

Both sides of Neck are worked at the same time, using separate yarn for **each** side.

Row 2: K1, (P4, K4) twice; with second yarn, (P4, K4) twice, P1.

Row 3: P4, K4, P4, K3, SSK; with second yarn, P2 tog, P1, K4, P4, K4, P2: 16 sts **each** side.

Row 4: K3, P4, K4, P4, K1; with second yarn, K1, P4, K4, P4, K3.

Row 5: Knit across to within 2 sts of Neck edge, K2 tog; with second yarn, SSK, knit across: 15 sts each side.

Rows 6-9: Purl across; with second yarn, purl across.

Right Shoulder Shaping
Row 1: Purl across, **turn**; K7, **turn**; P7.

Bind off all sts in **knit**, leaving a long end for sewing.

Left Shoulder Shaping
Row 1: P7, **turn**; K7.

Bind off all sts in **purl**, leaving a long end for sewing.

RIGHT BACK
Row 1: With **right** side of sts on circular knitting needle facing and using larger size straight knitting needles, bind off 6 sts, P1, (K4, P4) twice, K8: 26 sts.

Row 2: K5 (buttonhole band), P4, (K4, P4) twice, K1.

Row 3: SSK, knit across: 25 sts.

Row 4: K5, purl across.

Row 5: P2 tog tbl, purl across to last 5 sts, K5: 24 sts.

Row 6: K5, purl across.

Row 7 (Buttonhole row)**:** Purl across to last 5 sts, K2, [YO, K2 tog (**buttonhole made**)], K1.

Row 8: K5, purl across.

Row 9: Knit across.

Row 10: K5, purl across.

Rows 11-15: Knit across.

Row 16: K5, purl across.

Row 17 (Buttonhole row)**:** P3, (K4, P4) twice, K2, [YO, K2 tog (**buttonhole made**)], K1.

Row 18: K8, (P4, K4) twice.

Row 19: K1, (P4, K4) twice, P2, K5.

Row 20: K6, (P4, K4) twice, P2.

Row 21: P2, (K4, P4) twice, K6.

Row 22: K5, P2, (K4, P4) twice, K1.

Row 23: (K4, P4) twice, K8.

Row 24: K5, (P4, K4) twice, P3.

Row 25: Knit across.

Row 26: K5, purl across.

Row 27 (Buttonhole row)**:** Purl across to last 5 sts, K2, [YO, K2 tog (**buttonhole made**)], K1.

Row 28: K5, purl across.

Row 29: Purl across to last 5 sts, K5.

Row 30: Bind off 9 sts, P6, **turn**; K7.

Bind off all sts in **purl**.

Lapping buttonhole band over button band, sew bottom of bands in place. Sew buttons to button band opposite buttonholes.

Sew shoulder seams.

SLEEVE (Make 2)
RIBBING
With smaller size knitting needles, cast on 24 sts.

Row 1 (Right side): (K1 tbl, P1) across.

Row 2: (K1, P1 tbl) across.

Rows 3-6: Repeat Rows 1 and 2 twice.

Row 7: (Knit increase, K1) across: 36 sts.

BODY
Change to larger size straight knitting needles.

Row 1: Purl across.

Row 2 (Right side): Knit across.

Row 3: Purl across.

Rows 4-8: Knit across.

Row 9: Purl across.

Row 10: K4, (P4, K4) across.

Row 11: P3, (K4, P4) across to last st, K1.

Row 12: P2, (K4, P4) across to last 2 sts, K2.

Row 13: P1, (K4, P4) across to last 3 sts, K3.

Row 14: K3, (P4, K4) across to last st, P1.

Row 15: K2, (P4, K4) across to last 2 sts, P2.

Row 16: K1, (P4, K4) across to last 3 sts, P3.

Row 17: K4, (P4, K4) across.

Row 18: Knit across.

Rows 19-23: Purl across.

Beginning with a **knit** row, work in Stockinette Stitch until Sleeve measures approximately 6" (15 cm) from cast on edge, ending by working a **purl** row.

Cap Shaping
Maintain established pattern.

Rows 1 and 2: Bind off 3 sts, work across: 30 sts.

Row 3: SSK, knit across to last 2 sts, K2 tog: 28 sts.

Row 4: P2 tog, purl across to last 2 sts, P2 tog tbl: 26 sts.

Row 5: Knit across.

Row 6: Purl across.

Rows 7 and 8: Repeat Rows 5 and 6.

Row 9 (Decrease row): SSK, knit across to last 2 sts, K2 tog: 24 sts.

Row 10: Purl across.

Rows 11 and 12: Repeat Rows 9 and 10: 22 sts.

Row 13: Knit across.

Row 14: P2 tog, purl across to last 2 sts, P2 tog tbl: 20 sts.

Row 15: SSK, knit across to last 2 sts, K2 tog: 18 sts.

Row 16: P2 tog, purl across to last 2 sts, P2 tog tbl: 16 sts.

Bind off remaining sts in **knit**.

Placing center of last row on Sleeve Cap at shoulder seam and matching bound off sts at underarm, sew Sleeves to Romper.

Weave underarm seam (**Fig.** 19, *page* 39).

Sew buttons to button band opposite buttonholes.

COLLAR
LEFT SIDE
With **wrong** side facing and smaller size knitting needles, pick up 25 sts evenly spaced across Neck (**Figs.** 18*a* & *b*, *page* 39), beginning at center front and ending at center of button band.

Row 1: K2, purl across to last 2 sts, K2.

Row 2 (Right side): Knit across.

Row 3: K2, purl across to last 2 sts, K2.

Rows 4-7: Repeat Rows 2 and 3 twice.

Rows 8-10: Knit across.

Bind off all sts in **knit**.

RIGHT SIDE
With **wrong** side facing and using smaller size knitting needles, pick up 25 sts evenly spaced across Neck, beginning at center of buttonhole band and ending at center front.

Complete same as Left Side.

FINISHING
Matching bound off sts of front Leg Shaping, sew seam.

Repeat for back Leg Shaping.

FRONT SNAP BAND
With **right** side facing and using smaller size knitting needles, pick up 80 sts evenly spaced across front edge of Legs.

Row 1 (Turning ridge): Knit across.

Row 2: Knit across.

Row 3: Purl across.

Rows 4 and 5: Repeat Rows 2 and 3.

Bind off all sts in **knit**, leaving a long end for sewing.

Fold Band along turning ridge to **wrong** side and sew in place.

BACK SNAP BAND
With **right** side facing and smaller size knitting needles, pick up 80 sts evenly spaced along back edge of Legs.

Row 1: Purl across.

Row 2: Knit across.

Row 3: Purl across.

Row 4 (Turning ridge): Purl across.

Row 5: Purl across.

Row 6: Knit across.

Rows 7 and 8: Repeat Rows 5 and 6.

Bind off all sts in **purl**, leaving a long end for sewing.

Fold Band along turning ridge to **wrong** side and sew in place.

Sew socket side of snaps evenly spaced along **wrong** side of Front Snap Band; then sew ball side of snaps to **right** side of Back Snap Band.

TAM
RIBBING

With larger size straight knitting needles, cast on 74 sts.

Row 1 (Right side): (K1 tbl, P1) across.

Row 2: (K1, P1 tbl) across.

Rows 3-6: Repeat Rows 1 and 2 twice.

Row 7: K1, M1, (K2, M1) across to last st, K1: 111 sts.

BODY

Row 1: Purl across to last st, purl increase: 112 sts.

Rows 2-4: Knit across.

Row 5: Purl across.

Row 6 (Right side): (K4, P4) across.

Row 7: K3, P4, (K4, P4) across to last st, K1.

Row 8: P2, K4, (P4, K4) across to last 2 sts, P2.

Row 9: K1, P4, (K4, P4) across to last 3 sts, K3.

Row 10: K3, P4, (K4, P4) across to last st, K1.

Row 11: P2, K4, (P4, K4) across to last 2 sts, P2.

Row 12: K1, P4, (K4, P4) across to last 3 sts, K3.

Row 13: (P4, K4) across.

Row 14: Knit across.

Rows 15 and 16: Purl across.

Row 17: P2 tog, purl across to last 2 sts, P2 tog tbl: 110 sts.

SHAPING

Row 1: K1, (SSK, K 14, K2 tog) across to last st, K1: 98 sts.

Row 2 AND ALL WRONG SIDE ROWS: Purl across.

Row 3: K1, (SSK, K 12, K2 tog) across to last st, K1: 86 sts.

Row 5: K1, (SSK, K 10, K2 tog) across to last st, K1: 74 sts.

Row 7: K1, (SSK, K8, K2 tog) across to last st, K1: 62 sts.

Row 9: K1, (SSK, K6, K2 tog) across to last st, K1: 50 sts.

Row 11: K1, (SSK, K4, K2 tog) across to last st, K1: 38 sts.

Row 13: K1, (SSK, K2, K2 tog) across to last st, K1: 26 sts.

Row 15: K1, (SSK, K2 tog) across to last st, K1: 14 sts.

Row 17: K1, K2 tog across to last st, K1: 8 sts.

Cut yarn, leaving a long end for sewing.

Thread tapestry needle with long end and weave needle through remaining sts on Row 17; gather **tightly** and secure end. With same end, sew ends of rows of Shaping together.

BOOTIES
SOLE
With larger size straight knitting needles, cast on 19 sts.

Row 1 (Right side): K9, place marker, K1, place marker, K9.

Rows 2-6: K1, knit increase, knit across to within one st of first marker, knit increase, slip marker, K1, slip marker, knit increase, knit across to last 2 sts, knit increase, K1: 39 sts.

Rows 7-14: Knit across removing markers on Row 7.

INSTEP
Row 1: K 24, turn; leave remaining 15 sts unworked.

Row 2: Slip 1 as if to **purl**, P7, P2 tog, **turn**.

Row 3: Slip 1 as if to **purl**, K7, K2 tog tbl, **turn**.

Rows 4-12: Repeat Rows 2 and 3, 4 times; then repeat Row 2 once **more**.

Row 13: Slip 1 as if to **purl**, K7, K2 tog tbl, knit across: 27 sts.

CUFF
Rows 1-4: Knit across.

Row 5 (Wrong side): Purl across.

Rows 6-10: Knit across.

Row 11: Purl across.

Rows 12-15: Knit across.

Bind off all sts in **knit**, leaving a long end for sewing.

Sew back seam and Sole in one continuous seam.

ABBREVIATIONS

ch(s)	chain(s)
cm	centimeters
dc	double crochet(s)
K	knit
M1	Make one
mm	millimeters
P	purl
PSSO	pass slipped stitch over
P2SSO	pass 2 slipped stitches over
Rnd(s)	Round(s)
st(s)	stitch(es)
SSK	slip, slip, knit
tbl	through back loop(s)
tog	together
WYF	with yarn in front
YO	yarn over

SYMBOLS & TERMS

★ — work instructions following ★ as many **more** times as indicated in addition to the first time.

† to † or ♥ to ♥ — work all instructions from first † to second † or first ♥ to second ♥ as many times as specified.

( ) or [ ] — work enclosed instructions **as many** times as specified by the number immediately following **or** work all enclosed instructions in the stitch or space indicated **or** contains explanatory remarks.

colon (:) — the number(s) given after a colon at the end of a row or round denote(s) the number of stitches you should have on that row or round.

work even — work without increasing or decreasing in the established pattern.

KNIT TERMINOLOGY	
UNITED STATES	INTERNATIONAL
gauge =	tension
bind off =	cast off
yarn over (YO) =	yarn forward (yfwd) **or** yarn around needle (yrn)

Yarn Weight Symbol & Names	LACE 0	SUPER FINE 1	FINE 2	LIGHT 3	MEDIUM 4	BULKY 5	SUPER BULKY 6
Type of Yarns in Category	Fingering, size 10 crochet thread	Sock, Fingering, Baby	Sport, Baby	DK, Light Worsted	Worsted, Afghan, Aran	Chunky, Craft, Rug	Bulky, Roving
Knit Gauge Range* in Stockinette St to 4" (10 cm)	33-40** sts	27-32 sts	23-26 sts	21-24 sts	16-20 sts	12-15 sts	6-11 sts
Advised Needle Size Range	000-1	1 to 3	3 to 5	5 to 7	7 to 9	9 to 11	11 and larger

*GUIDELINES ONLY: The chart above reflects the most commonly used gauges and needle sizes for specific yarn categories.

** Lace weight yarns are usually knitted on larger needles to create lacy openwork patterns. Accordingly, a gauge range is difficult to determine. Always follow the gauge stated in your pattern.

KNITTING NEEDLES		
UNITED STATES	ENGLISH U.K.	METRIC (mm)
0	13	2
1	12	2.25
2	11	2.75
3	10	3.25
4	9	3.5
5	8	3.75
6	7	4
7	6	4.5
8	5	5
9	4	5.5
10	3	6
10½	2	6.5
11	1	8
13	00	9
15	000	10
17	---	12.75

■□□□ BEGINNER	Projects for first-time knitters using basic knit and purl stitches. Minimal shaping.
■■□□ EASY	Projects using basic stitches, repetitive stitch patterns, simple color changes, and simple shaping and finishing.
■■■□ INTERMEDIATE	Projects with a variety of stitches, such as basic cables and lace, simple intarsia, double-pointed needles and knitting in the round needle techniques, mid-level shaping and finishing.
■■■■ EXPERIENCED	Projects using advanced techniques and stitches, such as short rows, fair isle, more intricate intarsia, cables, lace patterns, and numerous color changes.

GAUGE

Exact gauge is **essential** for proper size. Before beginning your project, make a sample swatch in the yarn and needle specified in the individual instructions. After completing the swatch, measure it, counting your stitches and rows carefully. If your swatch is larger or smaller than specified, **make another, changing needle size to get the correct gauge.** Keep trying until you find the size needles that will give you the specified gauge.

MARKERS

As a convenience to you, we have used markers to help distinguish the beginning of a pattern or round. Place the markers as instructed. You may use purchased markers or tie a length of contrasting color yarn around the needle. When you reach a marker on each row or round, slip it from the left needle to the right needle; remove it when no longer needed.

KNIT THROUGH THE BACK LOOP (abbreviated K tbl)

Insert the right needle into the **back** of next stitch from **front** to **back** (**Fig.** 1), then **knit** the stitch.

Fig. 1

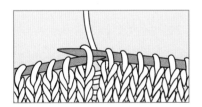

PURL THROUGH THE BACK LOOP (abbreviated P tbl)

Insert the right needle into the **back** of next stitch from **back** to **front** (**Fig.** 2), then **purl** the stitch.

Fig. 2

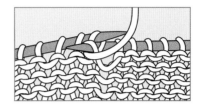

CIRCULAR KNITTING

When you knit a tube, as for the body of a skirt, you are going to work around on the outside of the circle, with the right side of the knitting facing you. Using a circular needle, cast on all stitches as instructed. Untwist and straighten the stitches on the needle to be sure that the cast on ridge lays on the inside of the needle and never rolls around the needle.

Hold the needle so that the ball of yarn is attached to the stitch closest to the **right** hand point. Place a marker on the right hand point to mark the beginning of the round.

To begin working in the round, knit the stitches on the left hand point (**Fig. 3**).

Continue working each round as instructed **without turning the work**; but for the first three rounds or so, check to be sure that the cast on edge has not twisted around the needle. If it has, it is impossible to untwist it. The only way to fix this is to rip it out and return to the cast on row.

Fig. 3

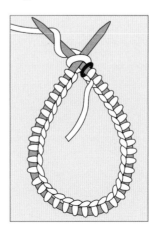

YARN OVERS

A yarn over (*abbreviated* YO) is simply placing the yarn over the right needle creating an extra stitch. Since the yarn over produces a hole in the knit fabric, it is used for a lacy effect. On the row following a yarn over, you must be careful to keep it on the needle and treat it as a stitch by knitting or purling it as instructed.

To make a yarn over, you'll loop the yarn over the needle like you would to knit or purl a stitch, bringing it either to the front or the back of the piece so that it'll be ready to work the next stitch, creating a new stitch on the needle as follows:

After a knit stitch, before a knit stitch

Bring the yarn forward **between** the needles, then back **over** the top of the right hand needle, so that it is now in position to knit the next stitch (**Fig. 4a**).

Fig. 4a

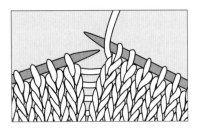

After a purl stitch, before a purl stitch

Take yarn **over** the right hand needle to the back, then forward **under** it, so that it is now in position to purl the next stitch (**Fig. 4b**).

Fig. 4b

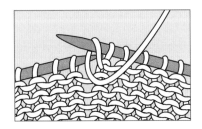

After a knit stitch, before a purl stitch

Bring yarn forward **between** the needles, then back **over** the top of the right hand needle and forward **between** the needles again, so that it is now in position to purl the next stitch (**Fig. 4c**).

Fig. 4c

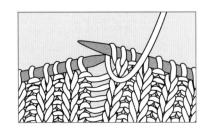

After a purl stitch, before a knit stitch

Take yarn **over** right hand needle to the back, so that it is now in position to knit the next stitch (**Fig. 4d**).

Fig. 4d

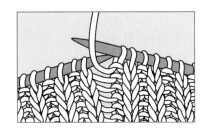

INCREASES
KNIT INCREASE

Knit the next stitch but do **not** slip the old stitch off the left needle (**Fig. 5a**). Insert the right needle into the **back** loop of the **same** stitch and knit it (**Fig. 5b**), then slip the old stitch off the left needle.

Fig. 5a   Fig. 5b

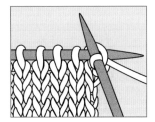   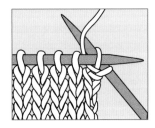

PURL INCREASE

Purl the next stitch but do **not** slip the old stitch off the left needle. Insert the right needle into the **back** loop of the **same** stitch from **back** to **front** (**Fig.** 6) and purl it. Slip the old stitch off the left needle.

Fig. 6

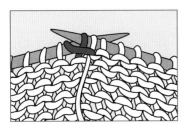

MAKE ONE (*abbreviated* M1)

Insert the **left** needle under the horizontal strand between the stitches from the **front** (**Fig.** 7a). Then knit into the **back** of the strand (**Fig.** 7b).

Fig. 7a

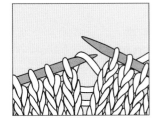

Fig. 7b

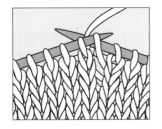

ADDING NEW STITCHES

Insert the right needle into the stitch as if to **knit**, yarn over and pull loop through (**Fig.** 8a), insert the left needle into the loop just worked from **front** to **back** and slip the loop onto the left needle (**Fig.** 8b). Repeat for the required number of stitches.

Fig. 8a

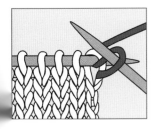

Fig. 8b

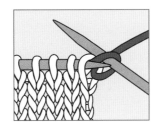

DECREASES
KNIT 2 TOGETHER (*abbreviated* K2 tog)

Insert the right needle into the **front** of the first two stitches on the left needle as if to **knit** (**Fig.** 9), then **knit** them together as if they were one stitch.

Fig. 9

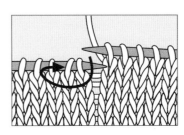

KNIT 2 TOGETHER THROUGH BACK LOOP (*abbreviated* K2 tog tbl)

Insert the right needle into the **back** of first two stitches on the left needle from **front** to **back** (**Fig.** 10), then **knit** them together as if they were one stitch.

Fig. 10

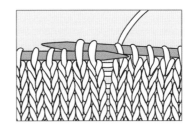

KNIT 3 TOGETHER (*abbreviated* K3 tog)

Insert the right needle into the **front** of the first three stitches on the left needle as if to **knit** (**Fig.** 11), then **knit** them together as if they were one stitch.

Fig. 11

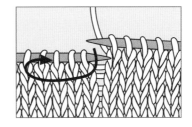

PURL 2 TOGETHER (abbreviated P2 tog)

Insert the right needle into the **front** of the first two stitches on the left needle as if to **purl** (*Fig.* 12), then **purl** them together as if they were one stitch.

Fig. 12

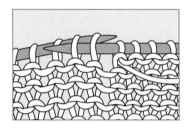

PURL 2 TOGETHER THROUGH THE BACK LOOP

(*abbreviated P2 tog tbl*)

Insert the right needle into the **back** of the next 2 stitches on left needle from **back** to front (*Fig.* 13), then **purl** them together as if they were one stitch.

Fig. 13

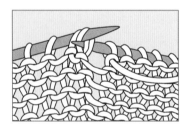

PURL 3 TOGETHER (abbreviated P3 tog)

Insert the right needle into the **front** of the first three stitches on the left needle as if to **purl** (*Fig.* 14), then **purl** them together as if they were one stitch.

Fig. 14

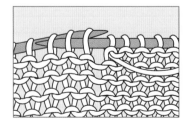

SLIP, SLIP, KNIT (abbreviated SSK)

Separately slip two stitches as if to **knit** (*Fig.* 15a). Insert the **left** needle into the **front** of both slipped stitches (*Fig.* 15b) and then **knit** them together as if they were one stitch (*Fig.* 15c).

Fig. 15a

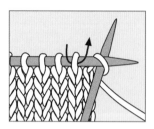

Fig. 15b

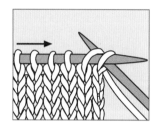

Fig. 15c

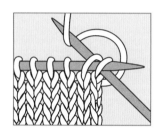

SLIP 1, KNIT 2 TOGETHER, PASS SLIPPED STITCH OVER

(*abbreviated slip* 1, K2 *tog*, PSSO)

Slip one stitch as if to **knit** (*Fig.* 16a), then knit the next two stitches together (*Fig.* 9, *page* 37). With the left needle, bring the slipped stitch over the stitch just made (*Fig.* 16b) and off the needle.

Fig. 16a

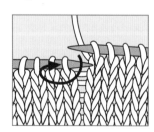

Fig. 16b

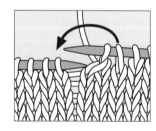

SLIP 2 TOGETHER, KNIT 1, PASS 2 SLIPPED STITCHES OVER

(abbreviated slip 2 tog, K1, P2SSO)

Slip two stitches **together** as if to **knit** (Fig. 17a), then knit the next stitch. With the left needle, bring both slipped stitches over the knit stitch (Fig. 17b) and off the needle.

Fig. 17a

Fig. 17b

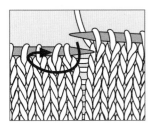
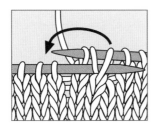

PICKING UP STITCHES

When instructed to pick up stitches, insert the needle from the **front** to the **back** under two strands at the edge of the worked piece (Figs. 18a & b). Put the yarn around the needle as if to **knit**, then bring the needle with the yarn back through the stitch to the right side, resulting in a stitch on the needle.

Repeat this along the edge, picking up the required number of stitches.

A crochet hook may be helpful to pull yarn through.

Fig. 18a

Fig. 18b

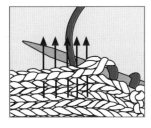
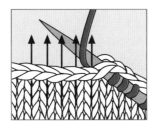

WEAVING SEAMS

With the **right** side of both pieces facing you and edges even, sew through both sides once to secure the seam. Insert the needle under the bar **between** the first and second stitches on the row and pull the yarn through (Fig. 19). Insert the needle under the next bar on the second side. Repeat from side to side, being careful to match rows. If the edges are different lengths, it may be necessary to insert the needle under two bars at one edge.

Fig. 19

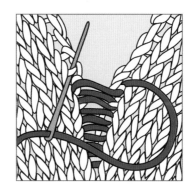

BASIC CROCHET STITCHES
CHAIN
Bring the yarn **over** the hook from back to front, catching the yarn with the hook and turning the hook slightly toward you to keep the yarn from slipping off. Draw the yarn through the loop on the hook (**Fig. 20**) (chain made, *abbreviated ch*).

Fig. 20

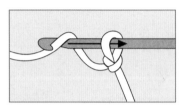

SLIP STITCH
To work a slip stitch, insert hook in stitch indicated, YO and draw through st and through loop on hook (**Fig. 21**) (slip stitch made, *abbreviated slip st*).

Fig. 21

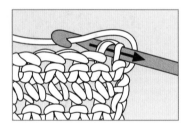

DOUBLE CROCHET
YO, insert hook in stitch indicated, YO and pull up a loop (3 loops on hook), YO and draw through 2 loops on hook (**Fig. 22a**), YO and draw through remaining 2 loops on hook (**Fig. 22b**) (double crochet made, *abbreviated dc*).

Fig. 22a

Fig. 22b

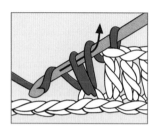 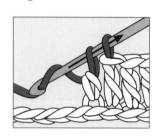

FINISH OFF
When you complete your last stitch, cut the yarn leaving a long end. Bring the loose end through the last loop on your hook and tighten it (**Fig. 23**).

Fig. 23

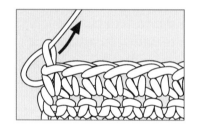

YARN INFORMATION

Each Christening Set in this leaflet was made with Red Heart® Soft Baby® #7001 White. Any brand of Light Weight Yarn may be used. It is best to refer to the yardage/meters when determining how many balls or skeins to purchase. Remember, to arrive at the finished size, it is the GAUGE/TENSION that is important, not the brand of yarn.

We have made every effort to ensure that these instructions are accurate and complete.
We cannot, however, be responsible for human error, typographical mistakes, or variations in individual work.

PRODUCTION TEAM:
Instructional/Technical Editors - Lois J. Long and Sarah J. Green, Editorial Writer - Susan McManus Johnson
Senior Graphic Artist - Lora Puls, Graphic Artist - Becca Snider Tally, Photo Stylist - Sondra Daniel, Photographer - Ken West

Instructions tested and photo models made by Margaret Taverner.